GARDEN
NOUVEAU
QUILTS

VICKY LAWRENCE

American Quilter's Society

P. O. Box 3290 • Paducah, KY 42002-3290

www.AmericanQuilter.com

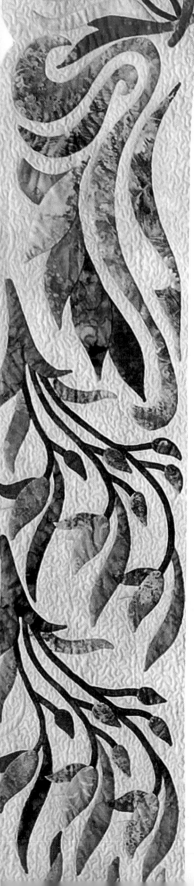

Located in Paducah, Kentucky, the American Quilter's Society (AQS) is dedicated to promoting the accomplishments of today's quilters. Through its publications and events, AQS strives to honor today's quiltmakers and their work and to inspire future creativity and innovation in quiltmaking.

Executive Book Editor: Andi Milam Reynolds
Additional Editing: Linda Baxter Lasco
Graphic Design: Lynda Smith
Cover Design: Michael Buckingham
Quilt Photography: Charles R. Lynch

Additional copies of this book may be ordered from the American Quilter's Society, PO Box 3290, Paducah, KY 42002-3290, or online at www.AmericanQuilter.com.

Text © 2009, Author, Vicky Lawrence
Artwork © 2009, American Quilter's Society

Library of Congress Cataloging-in-Publication Data

Lawrence, Vicky, 1948-
 Garden nouveau quilts / by Vicky Lawrence.
  p. cm.
 ISBN 978-1-57432-651-2
 1. Appliqu?--Patterns. 2. Patchwork--Patterns. 3. Gardens in art. I. Title.

TT779.L33 2009
746.44'5041--dc22

2009039482

American Quilter's Society
P. O. Box 3290 • Paducah, KY 42002-3290
www.AmericanQuilter.com

Contents

Introduction

Okay! Here we go on a fun trip into an earlier and more graceful time in our past as you make the Nouveau Fleur quilt or other items in this book.

These appliqué patterns are reminiscent of the art nouveau style from the beginning of the 20th century. Art nouveau captures a flowing style using organic motifs. The Nouveau Fleur quilt is made so you've got an entire bed quilt from nine designs, with four made twice. You will have a sense of accomplishment when you finish each block.

Every block is different so you won't become bored as sometimes happens when making a repetitive pattern over and over. You can start with any block or with the first one in the book—it's up to you. You are master of this quilt. Enjoy the feeling!

I started drawing when I was a child and loved it. As the years progressed, I took up quilting, making geometric blocks mostly because they were easiest and quickest, but they were boring after the first few blocks. Now I combine my love of drawing with my quilting by using appliqué.

At first I wasn't too thrilled with appliqué because I thought it was so slow and tedious. But I have finally figured out a technique that I can enjoy and is easy to transport. I get a lot more done on my appliqué quilts even though they are done by hand because I can do it anywhere—in the doctor's office instead of looking through the boring selection of magazines, in the airport while waiting for a plane (I do miss people watching though)—you name it. I really like to hand appliqué at the Civil War meetings that I sometimes go to with our family's re-enacting, and it fits the period.

It is so easy to get a block done in these snippets of time. I bet you will be able to find all kinds of little bits of time to work on your appliqué once you get started. It's addictive!

Supplies

You will need basic sewing supplies plus a few extras for the appliqué technique:

Freezer paper. Freezer paper has paper on one side and a plastic film on the other side, which will adhere to your fabric when pressed with an iron.

Pencil and eraser. I like a mechanical pencil because you have a sharp point at the "click" of the finger. Pink Pearl® Eraser is my favorite eraser for the paper part of this technique. It's cheap, available at any office or art supply store, and erases more mistakes than even I can make.

Appliqué needles. I like longer needles—straws and milliners—but there are appliqué needles, too. Any long, thin needle to get those tiny stitches that hide so well will do.

Wooden toothpicks. Square toothpicks are best because they have little fibers along the edges that grip your fabric to turn the seam allowance under. Your saliva will raise these fibers.

Tracing plastic and extra fine permanent pen or water-soluble marking pen. You can trace an overlay for your pieces layout on the plastic with the permanent pen or you can use a water-soluble pen to trace your layout directly onto your background. If you are using a dark background, the plastic layout is easier to see. Let the ink dry on the plastic to avoid smearing.

Appliqué-pressing sheet for fusible method. This is usually made of Teflon® or other non-stick material, protects the fabric, any fusible material and the iron, and is available at most quilt shops.

Very fine sewing thread. This is usually a silk thread or a two-ply thread such as machine embroidery thread.

Once, a very, very good appliquér told me that I really didn't need thread that matched my motif to the appliqué; if I were a "good appliquér," I could use blue thread on my gold circle in the center of my Mariner's Compass, and she was right. But I like to take every advantage I can find to get a good result without the strain, so, if I have a purple flower, I appliqué with purple thread. It saves some of the stress on me since I'm not the "good appliquér" I would like to be. [Editor's note: Vicky is too modest. Her workmanship is excellent.]

Appliqué pins or sequin pins. These are short straight pins, about ½" long, to pin your pieces in place without catching your sewing thread as you work.

Celtic or bias bar, ¼" & ⅛". I can make a lot of stems with these bars at one time and roll them on an empty thread spool to keep them under control and ready for the next block.

Sewing machine in good working order. Nothing is more frustrating than trying to sew on a machine that eats your fabric or just doesn't pull the seam through as it should.

Neutral sewing thread. Beige, tan, gray—all can be used in sewing your sashings, blocks, and borders.

Seam ripper. Okay, I'd like to think I'm perfect, but reality has proven otherwise.

Wooden iron or fingernail, optional. If you are using the faux needle-turn method explained on page 7, you will need something, not necessarily a hot iron, to break the thread memory and turn the seam allowance to the back. Bonus: wearing down your nail eliminates the manicure need for one finger.

Fabric Selection

All the yardage amounts in this book are based on 40" wide fabric. There are some fabrics out there that are wider and some narrower. Please be aware that you may have to make some adjustments if your fabric purchase is narrower than 40" wide. When looking for fabric for your project, there are several things to remember:

Have fun!!!!

Purchase the colors YOU like. It's much easier to work on a project you like than one where you hate the colors.

Remember that the backs of the fabric can sometimes be as interesting as the front. I wanted an antique, weathered background for one quilt. I found the back of a tan fabric gave me the worn look I was looking for.

I like batiks for the beautiful colors available, but they are a little more challenging to appliqué since they are so tightly woven. On the other side of the coin, since they are so tightly woven, inside points turn out much nicer because they don't ravel. Always rinse batiks until the water runs clear, as excess dye can be left in new fabric from the dyeing process.

Tone-on-tone fabrics will probably work better for this project than obvious prints. You don't want a teddy bear motif showing up on one of your flower petals. That is so not art nouveau!

Look through your stash. Since not all the flowers are the same color, you might find a scrap of that beautiful fabric you used and just couldn't part with the very last of it.

Use your imagination!

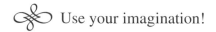

Appliqué Techniques

I'm going to discuss three types of appliqué—two by hand and the third, fusible.

Both hand techniques use freezer paper to create the shapes. Both yield good results and are very easy to take along. I do prefer one a little over the other but it's mostly because I have done it more and am a little more comfortable with it. The second has advantages, too. I suggest that you try both techniques and see which works best for you and then go to it and get lots done.

As you will notice on the layout of the blocks, there are numbers in the pieces of the motifs. These numbers indicate what order to place the pieces on your background.

As in all appliqué, rinsing your fabric first helps the freezer paper or the fusible stick to your fabric better. Rinsing takes out some of the sizing that seems to repel the paper from sticking as well as it should to your pieces.

I strongly suggest that if you are using any batiks in your project that you rinse them in warm water until they run clear. In making batiks, lots of dye is used and there will probably be excess dye that needs to be rinsed out before the fabric is put into your project. It would be a terrible shame if, when you rinsed out the water-soluble pen or when you first washed your quilt, the flowers bled onto your background! Other fabrics will do this too, so it is best to rinse all fabrics before using them in your quilt. You are going to spend time and money on this project and you deserve to have the very nicest end result possible.

Hand Technique # 1: Freezer Paper on the Wrong Side of the Fabric Technique or Faux Needle-turn Method

In this technique, you will need to reverse the patterns that are drawn in the pattern section of the book. Or you can just do it as it is shown and it will be reversed in the finished product. This won't matter, because all of these patterns are non-directional. If the flower sways toward the left instead of the right, it isn't a big deal, so you get to decide if you want to reverse or not.

With a pencil, trace the pieces of your motif onto the paper side of the freezer paper by laying your freezer paper over the pattern. A light box or bright window might make this tracing easier. Trace and label or number all the pieces.

I like to put an arrow pointing to the edge that is placed under another piece. Then I know that I don't have to turn this edge under to sew it down. It is left as is and the next piece lies over the raw edge.

Cut out your pieces of freezer paper on the drawn lines.

> *Note:* Both hand techniques are the same from this point on.

On the wrong side of your fabric, iron the freezer paper down. Be sure to put the shiny side against the wrong side of the fabric. If you don't, you will iron the paper pieces to your iron instead of your fabric. Believe me, this doesn't work and then you have to make the paper pieces again and clean the iron! Also, check that you like the position of the freezer paper on the fabric design before you iron (although you can remove the paper and use it again).

Cut around the paper/fabric pieces leaving a ⅛" to ³⁄₁₆" seam beyond the paper. This figure isn't critical. It shouldn't be wide enough to add bulk to your project, but it also shouldn't be narrow enough to allow raveling when turning your seam under.

I don't trim my points or inside curves at this time. I trim when I am ready to put a piece down to sew. I feel this keeps the fabric intact longer. If it is trimmed down to the final amount too soon, there is a chance of it raveling too much just from moving the pieces around.

I like to get all my pieces cut out for a block before I start sewing. Then I can put them all in a clear, plastic, closeable bag or a plastic project box for easy transport to sew at those odd down times.

Now, if you are using the overlay method, make an overlay with the plastic film by using the Sharpie® pen and drawing the entire layout on the film. Let the ink dry before you pick it up; otherwise, you will have black smears in some place you really don't want them.

As you become more adept at laying your pieces under the plastic layout sheet, you might be able to lay down more than one piece at a time. It takes a little practice, so don't rush.

If you are using the water-soluble pen option, you will draw the layout directly on your background. I've used both methods and either one works fine. See the tip on this page before marking.

When you are ready to start your appliqué, you may want to trim the points down a little so there is less to turn under. Also, on inside curves, make several little snips into the seam allowance. For an inside point, clip into the seam allowance almost to the freezer paper. Do this last prep work just before

you put the appliqué onto the block. It will keep the motif piece edges fresher so there is less raveling while you sew.

With the wooden iron or your fingernail, press the seam allowance under to the paper edge. This seems to break the fiber's "flat" memory a little and will make it easier to turn under as you work around a piece.

You will use a single strand of thread when appliquéing. Knot your thread and run it from back to front on your appliqué piece right at the edge of the freezer paper. By planting the knot on the motif

TIP:
If you have a dark background, you will probably have to use the plastic film. There are new marking products now that can show up on dark fabric, but a word of caution—test any type of marking product on a fabric scrap before going whole hog and drawing the complete layout on your background. It's better to know if the line will come out before you spend the time appliquéing a block only to find that the wonderful new pen won't come out of that particular fabric! I know because I had used a pen on fabric several times and had a great time with it. Then I used it on a special quilt border and it wouldn't come out. So the results will vary from fabric to fabric. Test, test, test!

piece instead of running the knot from the back of the background through the piece, you have the freedom to reposition the appliqué right up until you take the first stitches to sew it down.

Place piece number 1 down on your background with the knotted thread through from the back and start making stitches. Go down into the background and run under it to the place for your next stitch. Then come up and catch one or two threads along the edge of the appliqué piece. Now go right back down in the same hole you came up through in the background. By doing this, the only chance of your stitching thread to show is right where you took the stitch into the appliqué piece.

Continue stitching this way, turning under the seam allowance against the freezer paper's edge.

Okay, put the toothpick in your mouth to get it good and damp. (Now you look like a tough guy who appliqués.) When you get to an inside corner, you can use the toothpick to help tuck under the seam allowance. The dampness helps to open up the fibers in the toothpick; these grab the fabric and help turn it under.

When you have a point to work on, turn little bites of fabric under with your needle. Take smaller stitches toward the point. Once you are at the point, take a stitch there and then take another one to lock the point in place. Then start working down the other side.

On pieces that are not completely enclosed with a seam, pull the freezer paper out through the opening. On the pieces that are completely enclosed, slit the background and pull the freezer paper out through the slit.

After the piece is sewn down, take the needle and thread to the back of the background and tie a knot. You are ready to lay down piece number 2.

Hand Technique # 2: Freezer Paper on the Right Side of the Fabric Method or Traditional Needle-turn Method

When using this technique, there is no need to reverse the pattern. You will trace all of the pieces on the paper side of the freezer paper.

Cut out all of the pieces of the freezer paper on the lines.

On the right side of the fabric, iron the freezer paper pieces down. Be sure that you have the freezer paper with the paper side up before you press. You don't want to press the paper to the iron. Also, check that you like the position of the freezer paper on the fabric design before you iron (although you can remove the paper and use it again).

Follow the steps described in Hand Technique # 1 from here.

TIP: Don't use the water-soluble pen on the background, since ironing on your pieces may set the marks and make it unremovable.

Fusible Appliqué

For this technique you will trace the pieces onto the paper side of the fusible. Remember, if you want the block to be finished as shown, you will have to reverse the drawing on the fusible paper.

When tracing the pieces, be sure to leave some space between the drawings so that you can cut them out a little beyond the line.

Using the instructions for the brand of fusible you have purchased, set the iron to the correct temperature. Iron the fusible to the back of the appliqué fabric with the paper side of the fusible facing up. Otherwise, you will have to remake the pieces and clean the iron—not a fun job.

Cut out the pieces on the line.

Draw the layout on the plastic film to guide the layout of the pieces down on your background.

Peel the paper from the back of the pieces as you are ready to iron them onto the background. Lay a piece where you want it and then layer an appliqué-pressing sheet over the top to protect your iron. Iron the piece down and then remove the pressing sheet.

When you have all the pieces ironed down on the background block, machine stitch them down. Stitching makes the project much more durable. Set your sewing machine to a fairly narrow zigzag stitch. Shorten the length also. Practice on a scrap to be sure that your satin stitch covers the edge well. When you have it adjusted to the setting that you like, write down the numbers so that you can return to it without having to do a test sample again.

Making Stems

To enable the stems to make the graceful curves on this quilt, you will need to make them from bias strips. To find the bias of the fabric, fold it on the diagonal as you would for an old-fashioned headscarf: fold the cut edge to the selvage edge to form a 45-degree triangle. Cut off the triangle along this fold and set it aside or put it in your stash for future use.

For $\frac{1}{8}$" block stems, cut the bias strips $\frac{3}{4}$" wide. Fold these in half lengthwise with wrong sides together and sew a $\frac{1}{8}$" seam. Slip a $\frac{1}{8}$" Celtic bar into the strip. Roll the seam to the flat side of the Celtic bar so that when it is sewn on each side it will be hidden underneath. Press. If you have a metal bar, be careful to not burn your fingers when you slip the bar out. Then repress the stem without the bar to get a crisper edge.

For border stems, cut bias strips $\frac{7}{8}$" and use the $\frac{1}{4}$" bar.

I roll these strips onto an old empty spool to keep them flat, untangled, and ready for use.

Block Finishing Techniques

If you have used a water-soluble pen on the background of your block or another type of marking device, remove it at this time before you set an iron to the block. Follow the instructions for the particular product you used.

Since most appliqué techniques tend to draw the block up a little, extra has been added to the blocks on the outer edges so they can be trimmed down to the proper sizes. Once you have marking lines removed, trim your block to a size that will fit in your quilt. The trimmed size is stated on each block layout page.

The Nouveau Fleur Quilt

Machine quiled by Siriporn Hollar, Doublas, Kansas

Finished Size: 82" x 102" – depending on the number of borders you want on your quilt. Remember, you are the master here.

There are nine block designs. Their measurements are given as width x length.

Blocks 2, 3, 4, and 5 have been repeated to make enough blocks for the total quilt. You can make these

the same colors or you can do them with different colors. Some of my repeated blocks are different colors, some are the same. Your choice!

While you're thinking about fabrics and colors, note that you will need an inner border and three or more outer borders. NOUVEAU FLEUR has three outer borders; LITTLE VICKY, on page 68, has six. Fabric requirements will vary if you add or subtract borders or change their widths.

There are bumper strips on most but not all sides of the blocks. You can add them after trimming the block down to the correct size. There will be two measurements for these strips—you can sew them on with squared corners or you can make longer bumper strips and sew them with a mitered corner. Do whichever you are most comfortable with.

A size after the addition of the bumper strips will be given for each block. This will not be a finished size but the actual size ready to be sewn into the quilt. Use this measurement to check that the miter is correct, if you have decided to make the bumper strips with mitered corners.

Remember to rinse all of your fabrics in warm water to check for possible bleeding and to remove some of the sizing to make appliquéing easier.

Fabric Requirements:

Light block background: 2 yards
Light appliqué border background: 3 yards
Dark green bumpers, borders, and corners: 4 yards
Light green sashing strip and outer border: 3 yards
Flowers: Lots of small pieces of lots of colors
Swirls: 1 yard total of several colors
Stems: ¾ yard total of several greens
Leaves: ¼ yard total of 6 colors
Additional Borders: (optional) 3 yards of 2 colors
Backing: 2¼ yards of 108" wide fabric for 96" x 72"; 1⅞ yards for 86" x 62"
Batting: Queen or double
Binding: 1¼ yards. I always make bias binding because it wears better and hugs the outside of the quilt better. 1¼ yards gives you a square to work with. This means longer strips and fewer seams.
1 hank of embroidery thread for French Knots.

Bumper Cutting Chart

Block #	Cut	Size*	unfinished block size with bumpers
1	2	1½" x 8½"	10½" x 10½"
	1	1½" x 10½"	
2	4	1½" x 14½"	8½" x 15½"
	2	1½" x 8½"	
3	2	1½" x 24½"	25½" x 5½"
	2	1½" x 5½"	
4	2	1½" x 12½"	11½" x 14½"
	4	1½" x 11½"	
5	2	1½" x 14½"	9½" x 15½"
	2	1½" x 9½"	
6	1	1½" x 18½"	13½" x 20½"
	2	1½" x 13½"	
7	2	1½" x 28½"	12½" x 30½"
	2	1½" x 12½"	
8 (upper)	2	1½" x 4½"	10½" x 6½"
	2	1½" x 10½"	
8 (lower)	4	1½" x 10½"	10½" x 12½"
9	1	1½" x 18½	19½" x 20½"
	2	1½" x 19½"	

*Add 2" to the length if you want to miter the bumpers

Border Cutting Chart

Border	Cut	Size
Innermost	2	2½" x 66½"
	2	2½" x 50½"
Appliqué	2	9½" x 70½"
	2	9½" x 68½"
1st. Outer	2	2½" x 88½"
	2	2½" x 72½"
2nd. Outer	2	2½" x 92½"
	2	2½" x 76½"
Final Outer	2	3½" x 96½"
	2	3½" x82½"

Cutting

If you trust your sewing accuracy, cut the border strips first to take advantage of the fabric length, and cut the bumper strips next so that you have them ready to add to the blocks as you finish them. However, experienced sewers wait to cut borders.

Borders

See chart on page 12.

Note: Measure your quilt top for precise border measurements after you've completed the top, as everyone sews differently.

Bumpers

See chart on page 12.

Note: Measure your completed appliqué blocks for precise bumper measurements, as everyone sews differently.

Corners

Corners are cut using the marked corners on the block patterns and adding a seam allowance to turn under to appliqué to the blocks.

Block Backgrounds

Cut background pieces according to the cutting layout. 1½" extra has been added to the size of the actual blocks. After you are finished appliquéing the pieces to the block backgrounds, trim the blocks to the correct size (this eliminates any problems with drawing up during appliquéing). This trim will also create a nice new edge on your blocks after they've been handled a lot during the appliquéing process.

Note: The corner pieces on each block are appliquéd after the block is trimmed to the final size. Then the bumper strips are added.

Binding

Cut the binding 2¼" wide on the bias. Join strips together and press seams. Then press the binding in half lengthwise, wrong sides together.

Sewing the Blocks

You will use ⅛" Celtic bars for the stems in the quilt blocks. Use the ¼" bar for the border flowers. Appliqué the pieces for each block in numerical order.

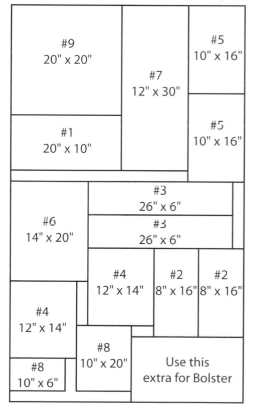

Block Background Cutting Layout

How to Miter Corners

You may want to miter the block corners instead of making squared-off corners. This is easier than a lot of people think. In the quilt, some of the blocks are mitered all around and some of the blocks only have miters on two corners.

First measures in ¼" from each side of the corner of your block. Put a dot lightly on the back at this ¼" place.

Lay your bumper or border flat on the table. Lay the 45-degree mark of a ruler along the edge of your border fabric and draw a pencil line along the edge. Stop the mark ¼" from the edge and make a dot.

Then do the same only in reverse on the other border that will be sewn to the same corner.

With a pin match the dot on the border with the dot on the block.'

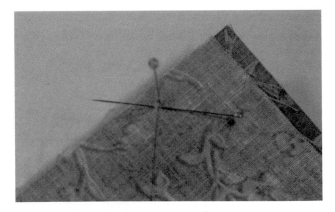

Now sew a ¼" seam along the edge and stop at the dot.

On the adjoining edge sew the border to the block, matching dots and stopping at the dot.

Now lay the two borders together matching the dots, and sew them together from the dots to the edge of the border along the drawn line. Then trim the excess corner off making a ¼" seam allowance.

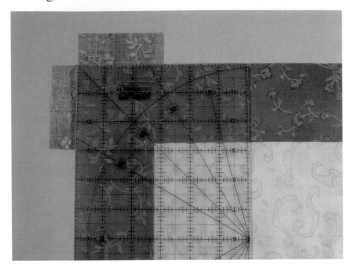

Open up and press the seam to one side.

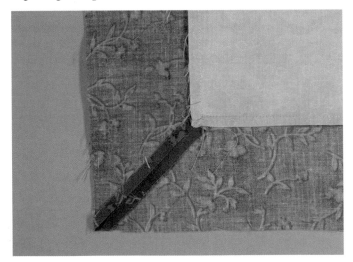

Photos courtesy of Bonnie Browning, from her book *Borders & Finishing Touches 2* published by AQS.

Block 1

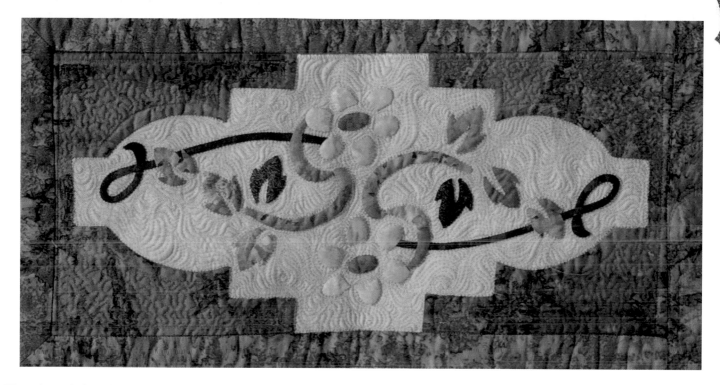

The dotted line is the center of the block. Turn the pattern 180 degrees to get the second half of the block. The corners are appliquéd.

After appliquéing the block, trim it to 18½" x 8½".

From the bumper strips, add a 1½" x 18½" strip to the top and bottom. Then add a 1½" x 10½" to the left side (if mitered, 1½" x 20" for the top and bottom strips and one strip 1½" x 12" for the left side).

After the bumpers are sewn on, the block should measure 19½" x 10½". If the block doesn't measure correctly, recheck your seams to be sure they are a true ¼", or recheck that you trimmed to the correct measurement.

Block 1

Connect Here

Block 2 (make 2)

The dotted line is the center of the block. Turn the pattern 180 degrees to get the second half of the block.

After appliquéing two patterns onto a background, trim the two blocks to 6½" x 14½". The trimmed size does include the corners (curves).

Cut four bumper pieces for each block: cut two 1½" x 14½" (if mitered, 1½" x 16") and sew to each side of the blocks. Then cut two 1½" x 8½" (if mitered, 1½" x 10½") and sew one to each end of each block.

After the bumpers are sewn on, the block should measure 8½" x 15½".

Embroider French Knots at small circles

Block 2

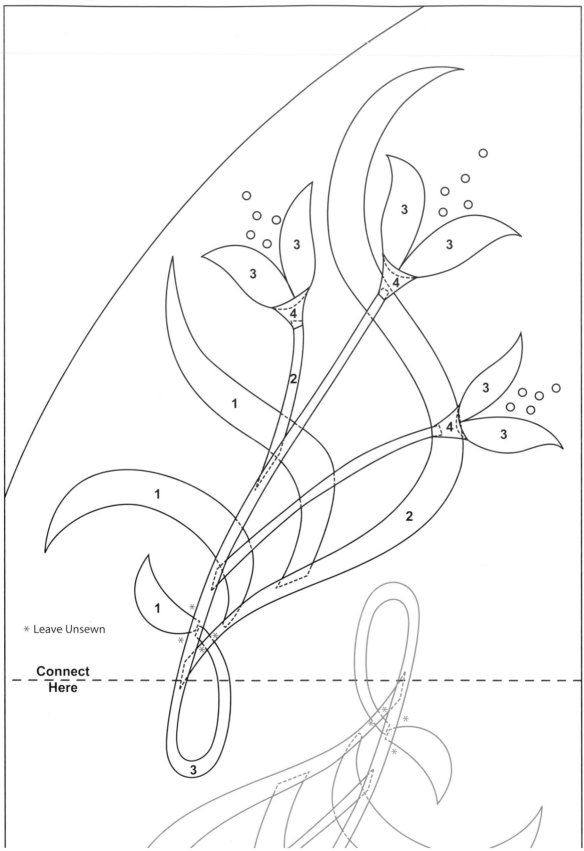

* Leave Unsewn

**Connect
Here**

Block 3 (make 2)

Join the pattern on the line marked "join." Turn the half block 180° at the centerline to make a completed block.

Trim the blocks to 24½"x 4½".

Add one 1½" x 24½" (if mitered, 1½" x 26") bumper strip to one side of each of the blocks. Then add one 1½" x 5½" (if mitered, 1½" x 7") bumper to the same end of each of the blocks. By adding them to the same side, they will become opposites when you turn one block in the quilt layout.

The blocks should measure 25½" x 5½".

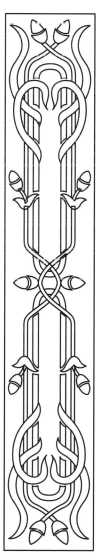

Block 4 (make 2)

The first half of the pattern joins at the dotted line. Then flip the joined first half of the pattern over to make the second half. This gives you the complete appliqué design.

Trim the appliquéd blocks to 10½" x 12½". Then appliqué the corners to each block.

Add the 1½" x 12½" (if mitered, 1½" x 14") bumpers to the left side of both blocks. Add one each of the four bumper strips 1½" x 11½" (if mitered, 1½" x 13") to the top and bottom of both blocks.

The blocks should measure 11½" x 14½". You will lay the two blocks as mirror images, one above the other.

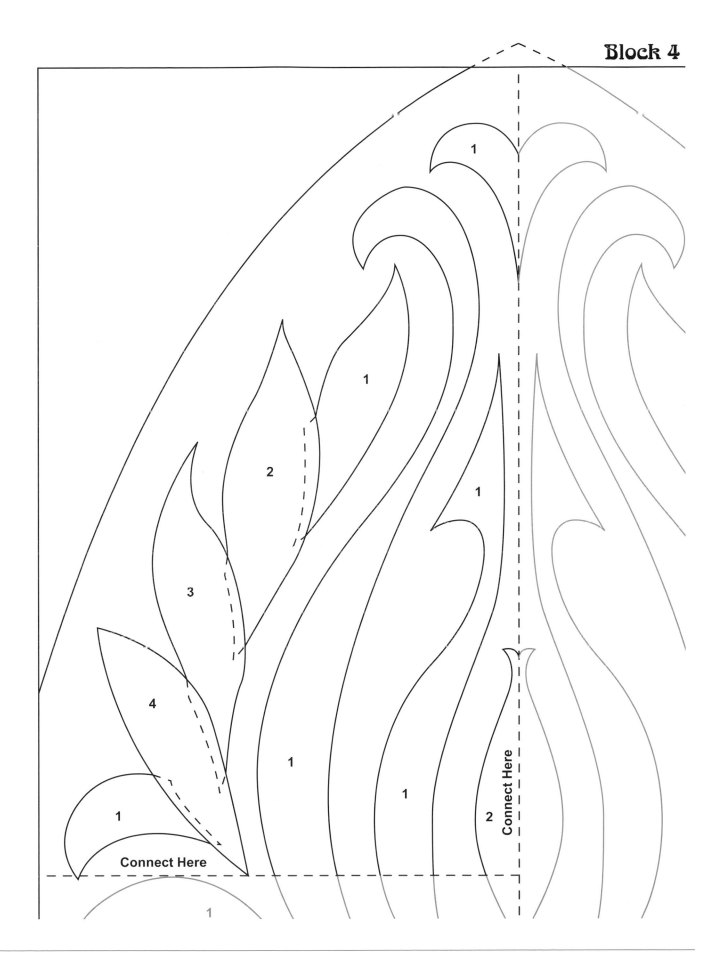

Connect Here

Connect Here

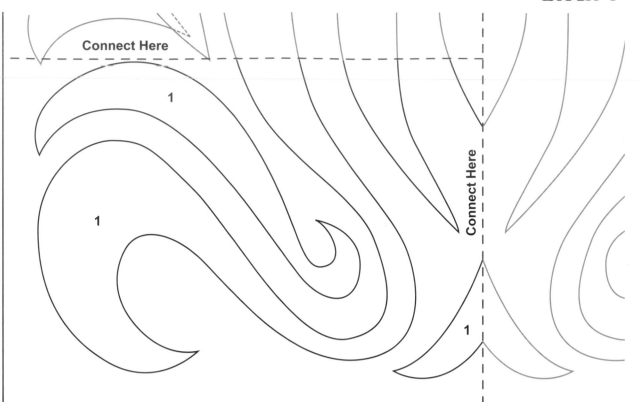

Connect Here

1

1

Connect Here

1

Block 5 (make 2)

Join the pattern on the dotted line. Then add the 4 corners.

Trim the blocks to 8½" x 14½".

Add a bumper to each block by sewing a 1½" x 14½" (if mitered, 1½" x 16") bumper on the right side of one block and the left side of the other block.

Sew on a bumper piece 1½" x 9½" (if mitered, 1½" x 11") to the top of the left-sided bumper block and the bottom of the right-sided bumper block.

Embroider French Knots at small circles if desired.

The block should measure 9½" x 15½".

Block 6

Match the dotted lines to create the full pattern.

Trim the appliquéd block to 12½" x 18½". Then appliqué the four curved corners.

Sew one bumper strip 1½" x 18½" (if mitered, 1½" x 20") to the right side of the completed block. Then sew one 1½" x 13½" (if mitered, 1½" x15") bumper strip each to the top and bottom of the block. The block should measure 13½" x 20½".

Embroider French Knots at small circles if desired.

Block 6

4   1   4   3   Connect Here   1

2

1

3

Connect Here

1

2

1

1

1

1

Block 7

This pattern is matched but flipped along the dotted lines. The bottom half of the block is just the reverse of the top half. Make two half blocks and join them to create one block.

Trim each half block to 10½" x 28½". Then add your corners.

Sew one 1½" x 28½" (if mitered, 1½" x 30") bumper strip to each side of the joined block. Then sew a 1½" x 12½" (if mitered, 1½" x 14") bumper strip to the top and bottom of the block.

The block should measure 12½" x 30½".

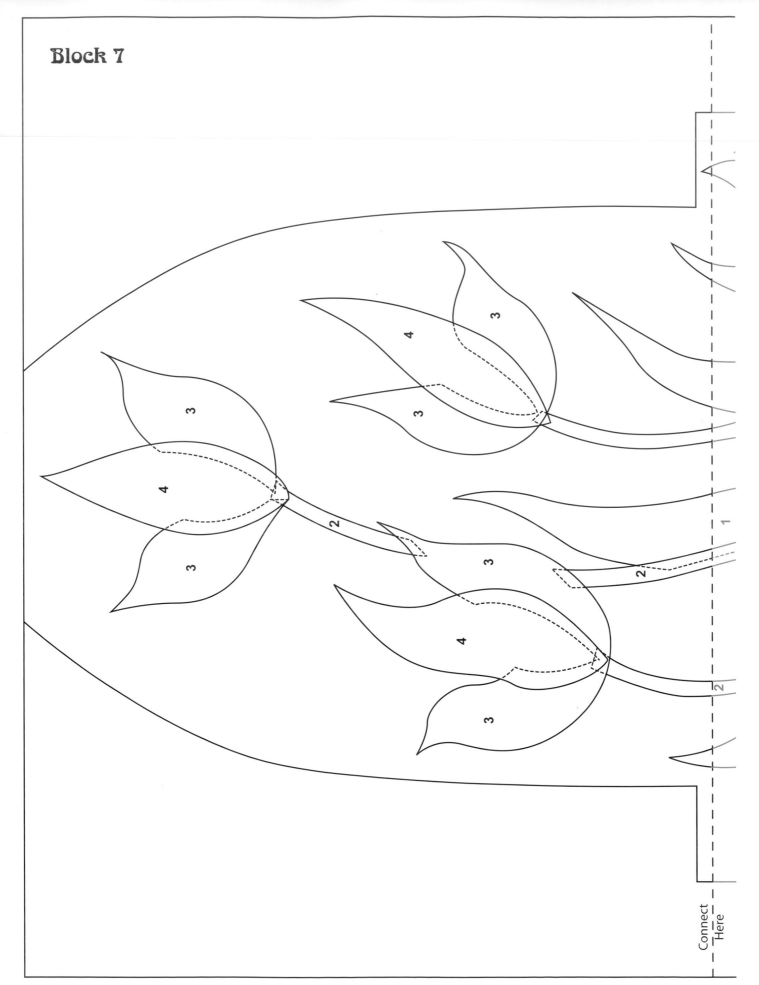

Garden Nouveau - Vicky Lawrence

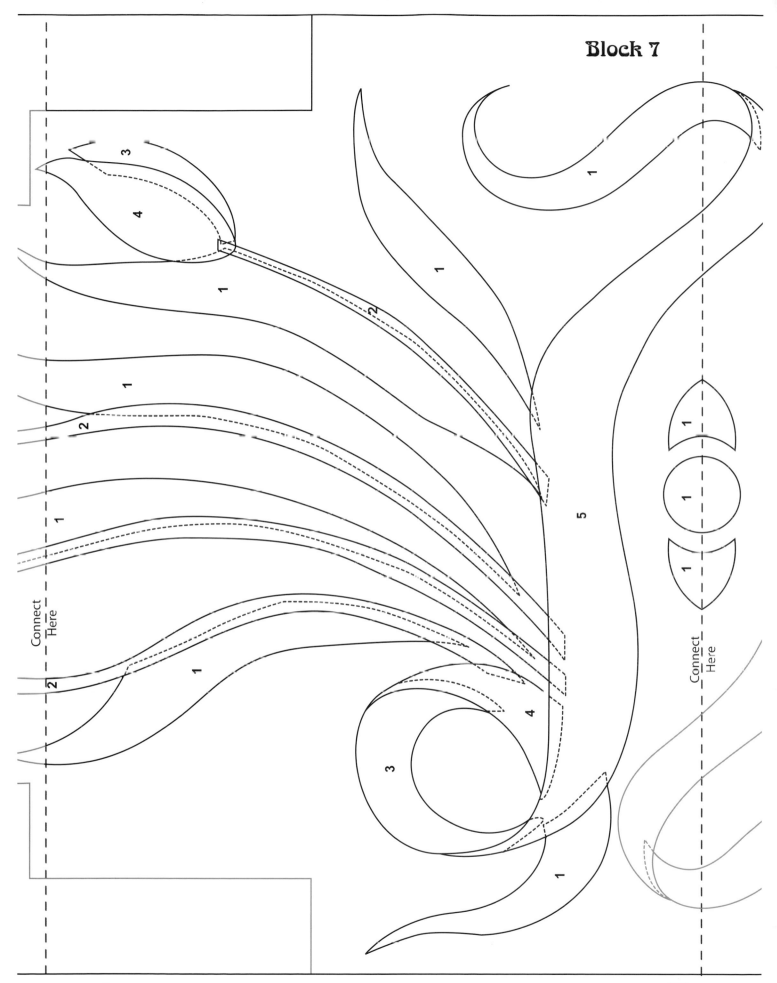

Block 8

This block has two sections. Join the lower section of the pattern on the dotted line. Trim the top portion to 8½" x 4½". The bottom portion will be trimmed to 8½" x 10½". Then add your corners to the bottom portion.

Sew a bumper strip 1½" x 4½" (if mitered, 1½" x 6") to each side of the upper section. Then sew a 1½" x 10½" (if mitered, 1½" x 12") bumper strip to the top and bottom of this section.

The upper portion of the block should measure 10½" x 6½".

For the lower portion, sew a bumper piece 1½" x 10½" (if mitered, 1½" x 12") to each side. Then sew on a 1½" x 10½" bumper (if mitered, 1½" x 12") to the top and bottom of the lower section.

The block should measure 10½" x 12½".

Block 9

Join the two pieces of the layout on the dotted line. This is a quarter of the block. Rotate this quarter three times to get the full block layout.

Trim the block to 18½" x 18½". Then add corner pieces.

Add a 1½" x 18½" bumper (if mitered, 1½"x 20") to the side. To the top and bottom, sew on a 1½" x 19½" bumper (if mitered, 1½" x 21").

The block should measure 19½" x 20½".

Block 9

Connect Here

4

3

1

1

4

3

1

1

4

3

1

1

2

1

4

1

4

Connect Here

Design Center

Borders

It is time to appliqué and add the borders. Congrats for getting this far!

NOUVEAU FLEUR can have five borders: If you do the appliqué border and the outer border your quilt will measure 96" x 72". You can stop the quilt before the appliqué border and your quilt will measure 86" x 62":

- the innermost border of dark green matches the bumpers and helps "float" the blocks;
- the appliqué border acts essentially as a block of its own;
- the third border matches the bumpers and corner fillers;
- the next-to-last border is light green and really frames the quilt; and
- the final border ties the dark green backgrounds, borders, and corners together.

The Innermost Border

To attach the first inner border around the outer edge of the quilt top, measure vertically through the center of the quilt. (Do not measure along the edge as it tends to stretch and give an inaccurate measurement for your strips.)

Cut two border pieces this measurement by 2½" from the long strips you put aside at the beginning (if mitered, add 4¾" to your measurement).

Sew one of these border strips to each side of the quilt top. Measure horizontally through the center of the quilt top and cut two pieces of this measurement from the reserved pieces (if to be mitered, add 4¾" to your measurement). Sew these borders to the top and bottom of the quilt top.

The Appliqué Border

Remember that you will use ¼" stems on the border flowers.

Cut your border appliqué background into four strips 9½" by the length of the fabric.

Appliqué the designs shown on pages 44–48 according to the photo on page 49. Note that the pattern is reversed and repeated.

Once the appliqué is completed, the actual border measurement should be obtained vertically through the center of the quilt top and the border trimmed to fit. For NOUVEAU FLEUR it was 70½", but differences in sewing by individuals could make this somewhat different for you.

To wrap the appliqué design around the corner as I did, you will have to center and divide the corner design and miter the border. To center the corner, draw an imaginary line from inner corner to outer corner, or if you are mitering your corners, the seam line will be the center of your corner layout. Measure vertically and horizontally through the center of the quilt. Use the mitering instructions to mark. Then sew and trim the excess.

To obtain the actual measurement of the appliqué side borders, measure through the center of your quilt body vertically for the side borders, and horizontally for the top and bottom borders.

To miter the corner, add 18½" to the actual quilt measurement for both top, bottom, and sides. Sew to your quilt. Miter the corners and complete the corner appliqué.

Repeat the measuring vertically and horizontally. Miter on your first outer border by adding 6" to your figure. Middle outer border, repeat the vertical and horizontal measuring and then add 6" to the figure you obtained. Add to your quilt and miter the corners.

The Outer Border

Measure vertically and horizontally through the center of the quilt. Using your mitering technique add your final border.

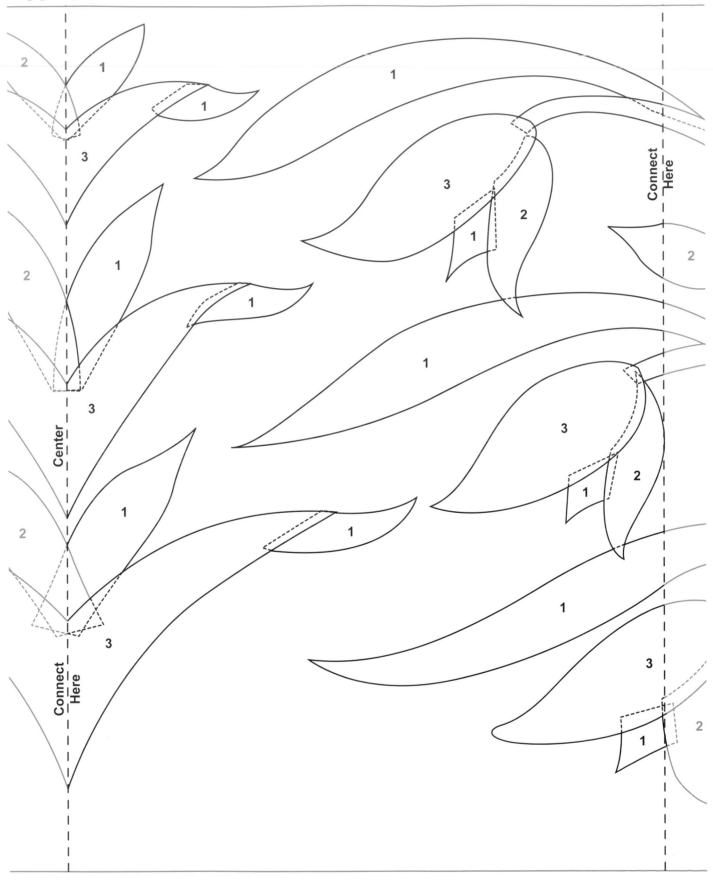

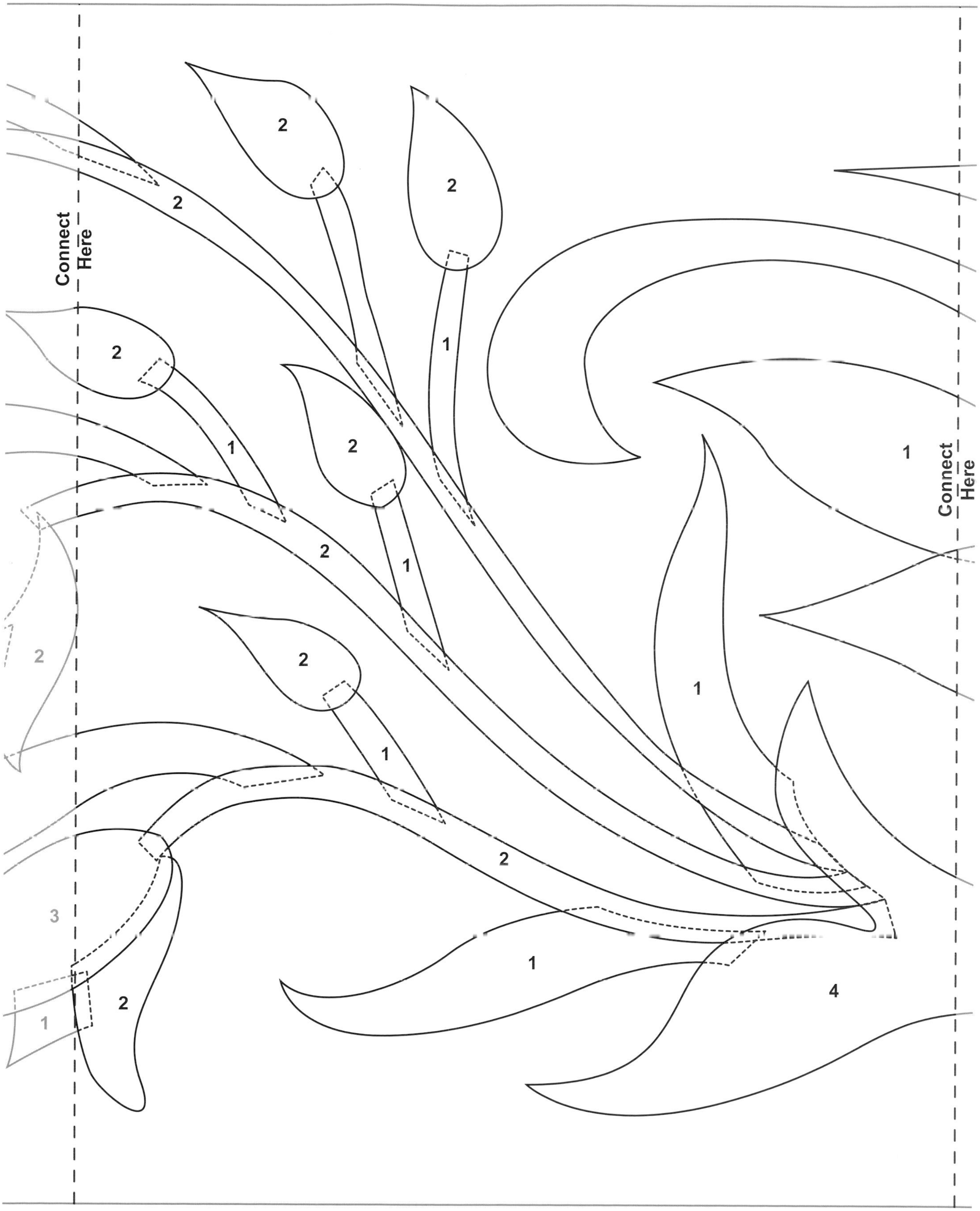

2

2

2

2

2

1

2

1

2

1

1

2

1

1

2

1

3

2

1

2

1

4

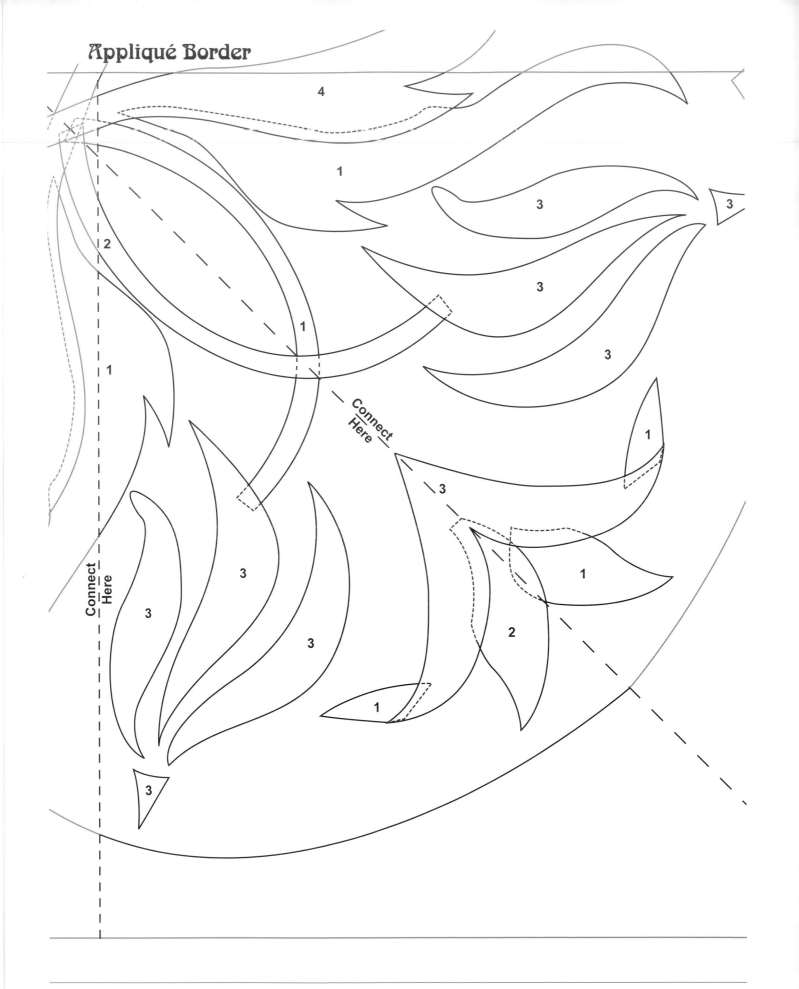

Connect Here

Connect Here

4

1

3

3

2

3

3

1

3

1

1

1

3

3

3

3

2

1

3

Top Assembly

Assemble the NOUVEAU FLEUR quilt top in four sections in a combination of bumpered (completed) blocks and sashing strips as shown on page 50 and the photo below.

The numbers in the sashing spaces are for the placement of the sashing pieces that you will now cut. All sashing strips are 2½", so when you see 15½" in the sashing space in the diagram, you will use a sashing piece that measures 15½" x 2½."

Construct each section of the quilt. Join the upper left and right sections together and the lower left and right sections together. Join the completed upper and lower sections together. Add borders and quilt as desired.

ART'S NEW BOUQUET
Made by Judy Robb, Manhattan, Kansas; quilted by Eula Long, Topeka, Kansas

Top Assembly Diagram
All sashing strips are 2½" wide

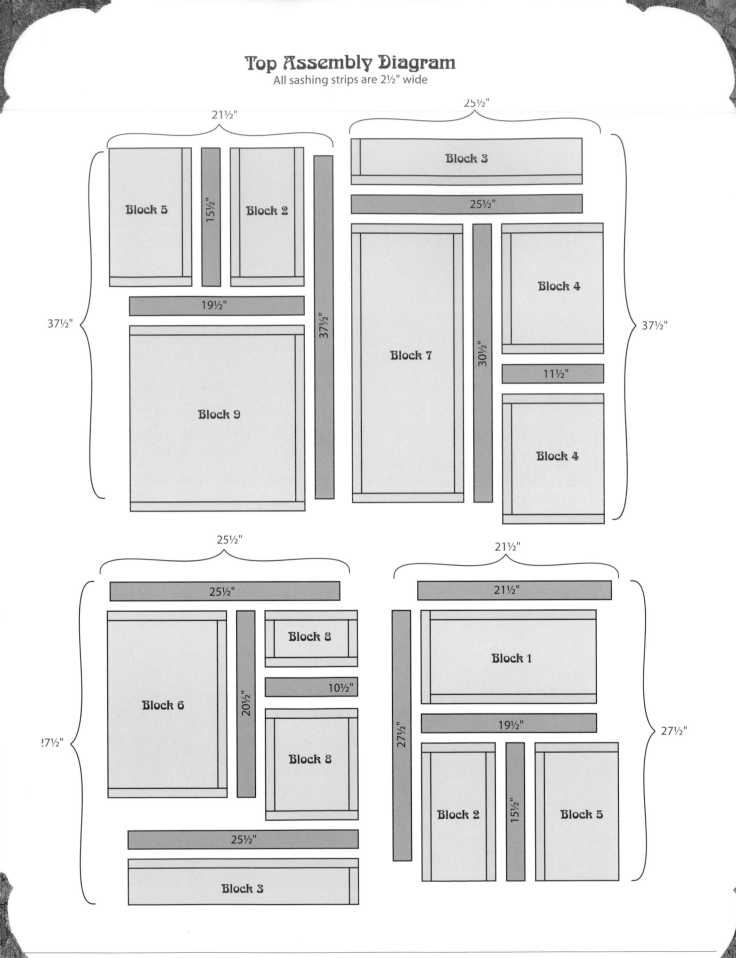

Bolster 24" x 8½"

Made by the author

Fabric Requirements & Materials:

Background: 1 piece 11" x 19"

Appliqué: ⅛ of a yard of at least 4 colors

Corners, sashing, back and rosettes: 1¼ yards

Backing (optional) 20½" x 12½" If you are going to quilt the bolster front you will need a piece of muslin 12½" x 12½".

Batting: (optional) 20½" x 12½"

Ties: 2 yards of cording and 4 end finishes (see side bar)

Pillow Form: 9" x 20"

Flip the layout at the center to complete one half of the appliqué design. Join the halves at the dotted lines to make a complete appliqué.

Cut 2 horizontal sashing strips 1½" x 18½"
Cut 2 end sashing strips 1½" x 12½"
Cut the back of the pillow 2½" x 14½"
Cut 2 rosette (end) strips 13" x 25½"

Sew sashing strips to all 4 sides of the trimmed appliqué piece.

At this point, you can quilt the appliqué front of your pillow, if you like. If you do quilt the appliqué section, measure it afterwards and re-trim as needed before you cut the pillow back, as the block will draw up.

Cut the pillow back to match the width of the trimmed appliqué front.

Sew the back to the top along the top seam. Sew a rosette piece to each side. Sew the bottom seam to form a tube. Press under ¼" on each outer edge of the rosettes. Fold to the inside and blind stitch the turned under edge to cover the seam where you attached the rosettes to the pillow front and back.

Slip the pillow form into the tube. Yes, it will be a little tough to do. No one wants a wimpy bolster, so the pillow form is really packed in. Center the form so the rosettes are of even length.

Cut the cord into two one-yard pieces and finish the ends. Gather up the rosettes and tie each cord into a bow. Pick and pluck at the rosettes until you have them fluffed up the way you want them to look.

An aglet is a sheath that covers cord ends to prevent unraveling (think shoestrings). They may be plain or fancy and made of precious metals, tape, wound thread, and anything else that will melt or bond the cord end fibers. A tassle can be attached to the cord end, as can buttons or anything you like to finish and protect the cord ends.

Sachet 5" x 5" x ½"

Made by the author

A sachet is a pretty and practical little item to freshen linens. It can be for you or given as a gift to a special friend. These directions finish at 5" x 5".

Fabric Requirements & Materials:

Background: 1 piece 6" x 6"

Corners: 1 piece 7" x 7"

Flower and leaves: scraps of several colors

Backing: 5½" x 10"

Inner muslin, if quilting: 6" x 6" and batting scrap

Lining to hold the fragrance: 1 piece 5" x 10½" (Some potpourri has oils and this lining bag will help protect your lovely appliqué.)

Potpourri amount: Small prepackaged potpourri or make your own.

Backing: (optional) muslin 6" x 6"

Batting: (optional) 6" x 6"

Embroidery thread: for French Knots

Use your preferred appliqué technique to create the front of the sachet. After appliquéing, trim down to 5½" x 5½". Appliqué the corners as shown in the photo. Now you can quilt the top if desired. Layer the top, batting, and backing and quilt. Trim to 5½" x 5½".

From the backing fabric cut 2 pieces 4½" x 5½". Make a narrow ¼" hem on the 5½" side of each piece.

Lay your appliqué face up. Place one backing piece face down, aligning the raw edges together.

Place the other backing piece face down on the stack, aligning on the opposite side's raw edges.

Sew a ¼" seam all around. Now turn the satchet right-side out. You should have an overlapping area on the back. Slip your fragrance bag in.

If you want to encase the potpourri in a lining, fold the lining in half wrong sides together. Sew a ¼" seam on the 2 short sides. Put your favorite smelling potpourri in the lining bag and baste the long edge shut.

Now just slip the fragrance bag into the satchet and tuck it under both pieces of the back.

Full-size pattern

Tote 16" x 15" x 5"

Made by the author

Fabric Requirements & Materials:

Bag background: 1 piece 22½" x 34½"

Bag lining: 2 pieces 15" x 26" and 1 piece 22½"x 34½"

Bag bottom: 1 piece 8½" x 22½"

Handles: 2 strips 4" wide x 44" long

Corners: 2 pieces 9½" x 4½"

Outside pockets background: 2 pieces 10½" x 10½"

Outside pockets lining: 2 pieces 9½" x 11"

Outside pockets matching trim: 2 pieces 1" x 10½"

Contrasting trim/binding: bottom of bag, 2 strips 1" x 23"; top of bag, 1 strip 1¼" x 46"

Flowers: scraps of five colors

Leaves: ⅛ yard total of three colors

Dots: scraps

One 1" *button*

Loop closure: 1 strip 1" x 8"

Stiffening with one side fusible: Note: Most stiffeners come in narrow widths, so you may have to piece strips together to achieve the size you want. To do this, abut ends cut at a 45-degree angle and connect them with a zigzag stitch. You will need enough pieces to get: 1½" x the length of the handles; 1 piece 17" x 34½"; and 4 pieces 2½" x 14".

Batting for outside pockets: 9½" x 10¼"

Inside pockets: 1 piece for trio pocket 15" x 18½" and 1 piece for duo pocket 13" x 15"

Zipper (optional)

Thread: neutral sewing thread and thread to match the appliqué, dots, trim, and binding fabric

Appliqué the two outside pockets in the method you have chosen. Trim both blocks to 9½" x 9½". Now appliqué the corners onto the block.

Sew one pocket trim to the bottom of each appliqué. Press the seam toward the trim. Then sew one pocket lining to the top of each appliqué. Press the seam toward the lining fabric. Measure up ½" from the appliqué portion on the lining fabric. Press a crease on the ½" measurement on the lining and fold the lining toward the back. Now you have a strip of trim at the top and the bottom of the appliqué. Slip the batting between the appliqué and the lining and quilt as desired. Set aside.

To make the bottom, press the bottom contrasting trim strips in half lengthwise and sew right sides together to a long side of your bottom piece with a ¼" seam, matching raw edges. Turn the trim seam toward the back and press. Repeat on the long edge of the other bottom piece. Set aside.

For the straps, iron ¼" under on each side of a strap piece, then iron the straps in half lengthwise. Lay the stiffener into the fold. Fold one ¼" over the other edge of the stiffener and then lap the other side on top. Stitch ⅛" in from the edge to seal everything inside. Then stitch the other side of the strap to match with a ⅛" seam. As an option, you can use one of your decorative stitches down the center of your strap. Live it up!!!!

Now you're ready to lay out the outside of the tote. Iron the large piece of stiffener to the back of the background, centering it 3½" from each side even with the top and bottom. Then iron the four stiffening pieces starting from the top and butting against the center stiffener piece.

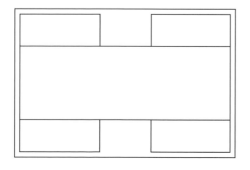

Pin mark the center of the bag background by folding it in half and pinning at the center. Do the same for the bottom piece. Lay the background flat right-side up. Lay the bottom on top, right-side up, matching the center pins. Pin through the center so that you can lift the trimmed edge to layer the pocket and handles underneath. Now lay the pocket with the lower edge ¼" under the bottom edge (not the trim but the bottom). Pin it down. Lay the handle along the sides of the pocket and ¼" under the bottom edge (not the trim but the bottom). Pin it down. Make sure you haven't twisted the handle. Stitch down the inner sides of the handles from the bottom edge up 12" to hold down the pocket. Then stitch on the outer edge of the handle to match. You will want to match your thread to the color of your handle when doing the stitching down to hold the pocket. It doesn't hurt to recheck your measurements to be sure the bottom will cover the raw edges of your handles and pocket before you sew just to be sure. It's easier to repin than to rip out.

Repeat with the other side of the bag. Flip the edges of the bottom back into place and pin along the edge. Rethread your machine with thread to match the trim and stitch in the ditch along the edge where the trim joins the back. That will join the trimmed bottom to the bottom of your bag. This seam should cover the bottom of your pocket and your handles.

Turn the bag so that the outsides are together. Pin. Stitch a ¼" seam down the sides. Then fold the lower corner into a point. Measure to mark a 6" seam line by laying your large ruler on the point and move it until the edge measures 6". You can check to be sure the line is square by making sure the side seam runs directly down a straight mark on your ruler. Mark with a pencil. Then stitch along this line. Repeat with the other side.

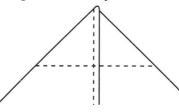

Turn the tote bag right-side out. At this point, you may want to make a permanent crease at the corners. To do this, fold at the corner and stitch a seam ⅛" in along the crease. Repeat for the other three corners.

Now work on the lining and inside trio pocket. Fold the inside trio pocket piece in half right sides together to form a piece 15" x 9¼". Sew a ¼" seam on each side. Turn right-side out. Repeat with the duo pocket.

Mark the center of the lining across the bottom with a crease. Measure up 3¼" and mark a faint line. Repeat for the other side of the center.

Lay the pockets with raw edges along the drawn line making sure to have the pocket toward the center and the right sides together. Sew a ¼" seam and flip the pocket up to cover the raw edge. To make a large single pocket, top stitch along both side edges of your pocket and you're done. To make a duo pocket, mark a division at the center of your pocket and sew from the top to the bottom of the pocket to make two pockets out of the one. Divide the pocket in thirds, approximately, and sew from the top of the pocket to the bottom to make a trio pocket.

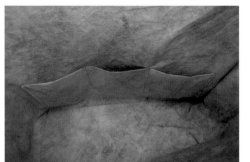

Trio pocket

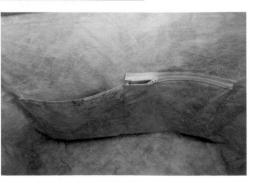

Duo pocket

Next, with right sides together sew down each side of the lining. Fold the corner as you did for the outside of the bag and sew a 6" seam across both corners.

Slip the lining into the bag. Make sure you can see the pockets in the bag to be sure you don't have the lining wrong-side out.

Now how about a latch? Fold the 1" x 8" piece in half lengthwise and press. Then fold both edges under ¼". Stitch to seal.

Fold in half and flatten the point to make an arrow shape to be sure you haven't twisted your strip.

You're almost there! Join the two pieces of your binding with a bias seam—it reduces bulk.

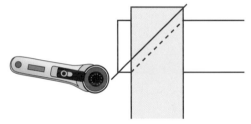

Press the seam to one side. Then press and fold the binding in half lengthwise to a fine, crisp edge.

With raw edges together, stitch the binding to the inside of the bag being sure to catch the lining, binding, and outside of the bag. Fold under the starting end and lap over the folded end for a finished edge. Turn the stitched binding to the outside of the bag, pinning the raw edges of the latch closure even with the binding raw edge in the center of one of the bag's long sides. Top stitch (or use a fancy stitch) the binding in place, catching the latch as you sew.

Pull the latch to the opposite side of the bag to determine the button placement. Sew the button on.

Yea!!! You are finished and have a nice tote bag for your goodies.

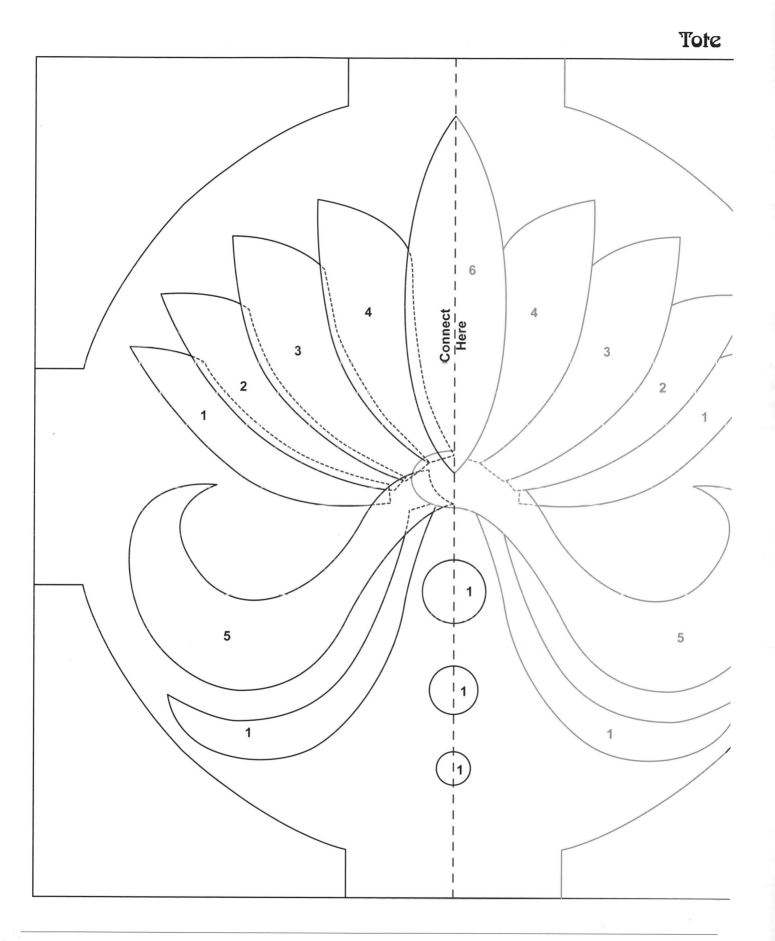

Connect Here

6

4

3

2

1

4

3

2

1

5

5

1

1

1

1

1

1

Table Runner 12½" x 30"
Made by the author

Fabric Requirements & Materials:
Background: 1 piece 22" x 11"
Corners: ½ yard
Edges: 2 strips 23" x 1½" and 1 strip 12½" x 1½"
Ends: 1 piece 4½" x 13". Cut 2 from the pattern on page 61. Make a mirror image of the template and join on the center dotted line to get a complete shape.
Leaves and buds: scraps of 3 colors
Stems: 1 fat eigth
Flowers: 2 shades of 3 colors – one 4" x 5" piece each
Backing: ½ yard
Batting: 34" x 16"

Join the appliqué layout on the dotted lines. Turn the pattern 180° to complete the design.

Appliqué the design on the background piece.

Trim to 23" x 10½".

Appliqué the corner pieces.

Sew an end section to each end. Press the seams toward the end pieces.

Lay the batting on a table. Lay the backing right-side up on top of the batting. Then lay the top of the runner wrong-side up. Pin around the edges to prevent slippage when sewing.

Sew a seam around the project ¼" in from the edge. Leave 6½" unsewn along one side to allow for turning the table runner right-side out. Trim the batting as close to the seam as possible without cutting into the seam. Now, trim the backing to match the top. Clip the excess from the corners in the seam allowance to reduce bulk. Clip into the seam on the curves to help ease when turned. Make sure not to clip into your seam line.

Turn the runner right side-out through the unsewn side seam. Smooth out edges and corners. You might want to lightly press the unsewn edge to make it a little smoother.

Slip stitch the side seam closed.

Pin-baste in several places to prevent shifting during quilting.

Quilt as desired.

Yea!! You have a table runner.

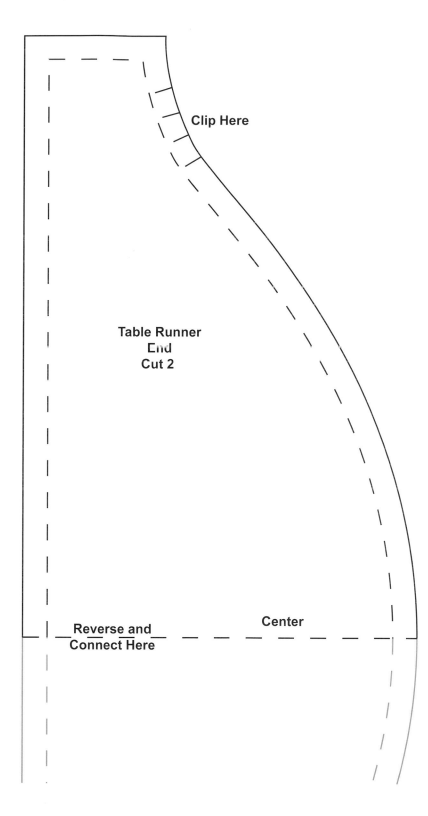

Clip Here

Table Runner
End
Cut 2

Center

**Reverse and
Connect Here**

Wallhanging 9½" x 22½"

Made by the author

Swirl: 8" x 12"
Flowers and leaves: scraps
Backing: ⅓ yard
Batting: 12" x 25" (very thin)

The layout is in 2 pieces. You will need to join them together along the dotted line to make a complete pattern layout.

Appliqué the design. Trim the piece to 8" x 15½". Appliqué the 2 corner pieces.

Sew a side edge to each side of the wallhanging. Press the seams toward the edge fabric.

Sew the 10" x 3½" strip to the top and an end piece to the bottom. Press the seams toward the border fabric.

Lay the batting on the table, and then lay the backing on top, right-side up.

Lay the top on the stack wrong-side up, but measure up 1" on the top edge. Start your backing at this 1" mark. This extra 1" will make the tube (sleeve) for hanging the piece on a dowel.

Sew around both sides and the bottom, leaving the top open for turning.

Trim the batting as near the stitching line as possible. You will want to clip the seam on the curve on each side of the end piece to make a smoother seam line when turned. Turn the wallhanging right-side out.

Quilt any way you want; you are the master.

9. At the 1" edge of the top, turn ¼" under and press. Then turn this flap to the back and attach as you would for a sleeve.

I think making two of these and hanging them side by side at different levels would be cool. Or, try reversing one to be a reflection of the image of the other.

Fabric Requirements (given for one only)

Background: 1 piece 17" x 9"
Corners, edges, and end: ¼ yard
Side edges: 2 pieces 15½" x 1½"
Top edge: 10" x 3½" Note: This will make your hanging sleeve too.
Bottom end: cut from template
Corners: cut from layout

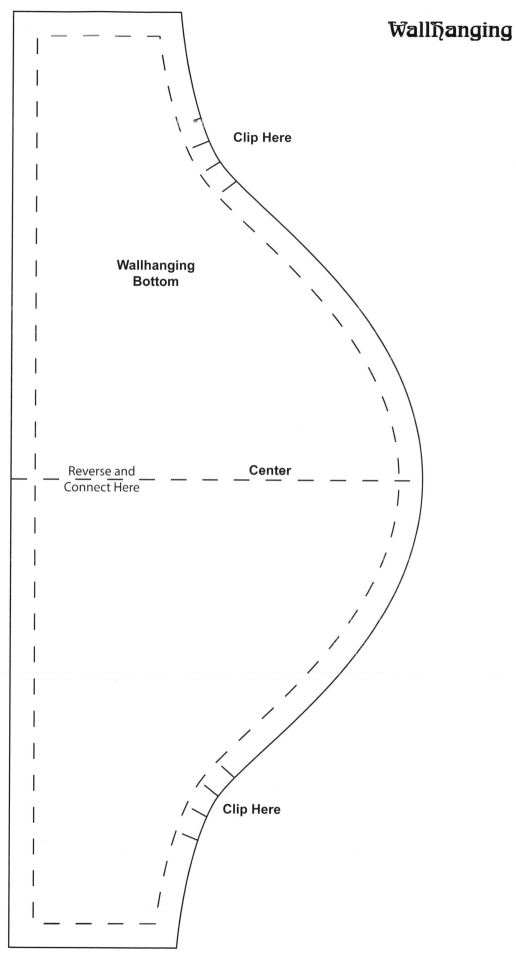

Clip Here

**Wallhanging
Bottom**

Reverse and
Connect Here   **Center**

Clip Here

WallHanging

7

6

7

6

1

**Connect
Here**

8

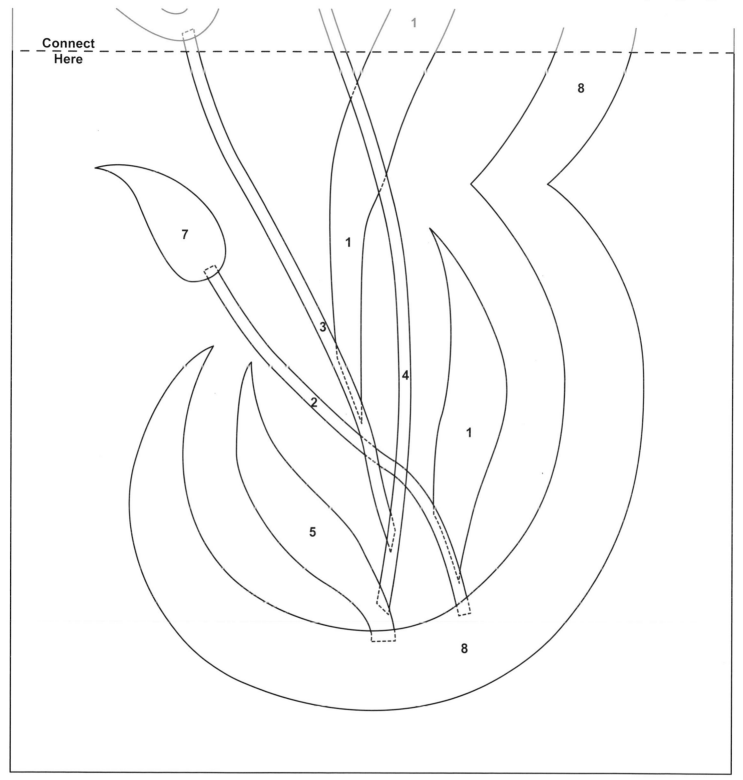

Connect Here

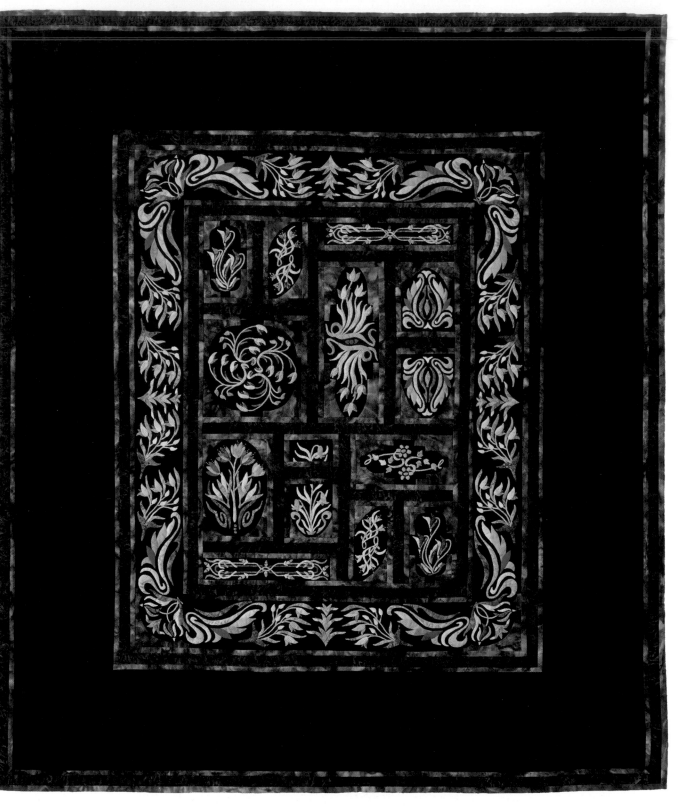

LITTLE VICKY
Made by Jill Burton, Silver Lake, Kansas

This exquisite miniature quilt is not for the faint hearted! LITTLE VICKY was created by reducing all of the patterns to one third the original size. One item you will need is a very good lighting system.

Fabric requirements

Background: 1½ yards
Sashing: ¾ yard
Flowers: fat ⅛ at the most
Leaves: ⅛ of several colors
Borders: 1½ yard
Batting: 30" x 30"
Binding: ½ yard

Remember that all your blocks will be ⅓ the size of the large quilt. For example, if a block is 6" x 9" in the large quilt, it will be 2" x 3" in this quilt.

Note:
Make the quilt in the same manner as with all the other blocks, reducing everything to 33% of the original.

Cut the bumpers around the blocks ¾" wide.

Cut sashings 1⅛" wide.

Keep all your pieces together for a single block in a plastic bag. These are tiny pieces and they stray very easily.

After assembling the quilt top, you get to decide just how large you will make your quilt. You can stop at the border just beyond the appliqué border. Or you can decide to add several other borders.

Cutting:

1st border beyond appliqué - cut 4 strips ¾" x length of fabric
2nd border - cut 4 strips 1⅛" x length of fabric
3rd border - cut 4 strips ¾" x length of fabric
You can stop here for the smaller quilt of 20" x 26"
Or continue for the larger quilt of 26" x 28".
4th border - cut 4 strips 6½" x length of fabric
5th border - cut 4 strips ¾" x length of fabric
6th border - cut 4 strips 1⅛" x length of fabric

The larger plain border has been added so you may add fancy quilting patterns. Always remember when adding your borders to measure the exact size of your quilt through the center before each addition. The variation from sewing machine to sewing machine or piecer to piecer will allow for some variation from the stated sizes.

Not to dissuade you, but appliquéing pieces this small is a real challenge. My suggestion is that you make the larger quilt or some of the projects to become very familiar with the technique before you tackle this miniature masterpiece.

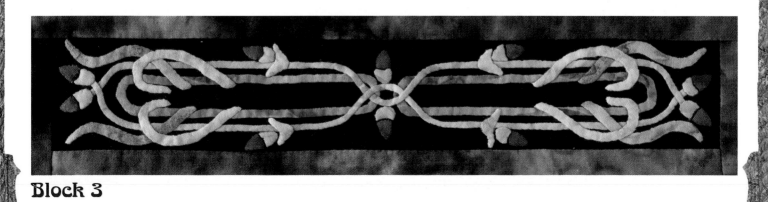

Block 3

Block 5

Block 5

Block 1

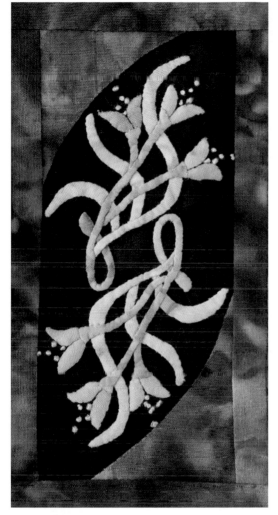

Block 2

Block 2

Block 7

Block 9

Block 3

Block 4

Block 8 (top)

Block 6

Block 8 (bottom)

Border Corner

Garden Nouveau - Vicky Lawrence

Border

Border

Border

Border Corner

About the Author

Photo by Jack Coppoc, Coppoc Digital

Little did I know back when I was a kid and drawing on anything and everything I could, including using lipstick on my mom's dresser, that it would lead to designing quilts. Here's what happened:

My husband, Dennis, and I both had grown up on farms, so purchasing a farm near Overbrook, Kansas, after we married was only natural. Since I spin, weave, and sew, raising the animals to produce fiber along with the Arabian horses that we love was also natural.

When remodeling our old (late 1800s) farmhouse, we purchased an iron bed at an auction. It needed a quilt (naturally), and so my journey as a quilter began.

After working at a bank for 29 years, where I used my drawing abilities to make cartoons in our employee newsletter and to draw ads for the local paper, I put my love of drawing and sewing to use by creating my pattern business, Prairie's Edge Patchworks. The original appliqué patterns in this book combine the nature that is around our home every day and my love of drawing and sewing.

I seem to have come full circle, and hope you enjoy the results.

Vicky Lawrence

 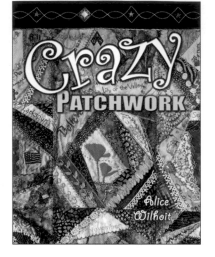 
 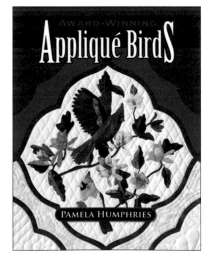